PUBLIC SPEAKING ESSENTIALS

SIX STEPS TO SIZZLE ON STAGE

RAMAKRISHNA REDDY

Disclaimer

While all attempts have been made to verify the information provided in this publication, neither the author nor the publisher assumes any responsibility for errors, omissions, or contrary interpretations of the subject matter herein.

This book is for informational purpose only. The views expressed are those of the author alone, and should not be taken as expert instruction or commands. The reader is responsible for his or her own actions.

Adherence to all applicable laws and regulations, including international, federal, state, and local governing professional licensing, business practices, advertising, and all other aspects of doing business in the US, India or any other jurisdiction is the sole responsibility of the purchaser or reader.

ALSO BY RAMAKRISHNA REDDY

Connect Using Humor and Story

Toastmaster's Secret

Public Speaking Topic Secrets

The Ultimate Public Speaking Survival Guide

Write Effective Emails at Work

Confessions of a Software Techie

Dedication

Dedicated to Jerry Aiyathurai, my mentor

Table of Contents

Introduction

If you are new to public speaking, I am so excited that you picked this book. In today's world, public speaking is not an option but a necessity. It's a skill that has many applications. One by-product of this skill is confidence and I feel excited to help you in this journey.

My own journey concerning public speaking began when I was in the third grade. Let me take you to the day when the stage was set for a speech contest. The auditorium was jam-packed. I was called to the stage. I held the mike. I started to speak, "Hello, time and tide waits for no man. So we should, so we should, um, ah, um, I mean...........thank you." It was one of the most embarrassing moments of my life. In the same contest, my classmate gave a splendid talk. I remember saying to myself, "Loser... Everybody in the school will mock you." I asked myself, "If he can, why can't I?" The fact was – I had FEARS. I was really scared to face hundreds of people from the stage. I wanted to overcome this fear. But I never took any real action. Time passed. I graduated and got a job. Only after I started my career did I realize the importance of speaking and communication. For a few years, I struggled with my discouraging self-talk, ego and anxiety. Then, I got excited about competing in a speech contest. I gave the best speech of my life (at least, I thought so!). I waited to be declared a winner but didn't even place in the top three. And this happened more than once. Oops! My ego hurt, my confidence hurt and my belief hurt.

So I knew I needed to take steps to overcome this situation and the first step I took was *to be coachable.* I read books, observed great speakers and reached out for help. The one person who changed my perception of public speaking was Jerry Aiyathurai, an amazing speaker and a genuine human being who also became a fantastic mentor to me. Had it not been for him, I would not have succeeded. Ultimately I won more than 25 public speaking contests ranging from entertaining to inspiring speeches. Despite being a non-native speaker, I placed among the top three speakers in the New England area of the United States. I also placed in the top three twice in a row at the India level in speech contests. Today, because of my experiences in learning public speaking, I have to laugh as I think back on what I thought I knew when I was new to the craft of public speaking. It turns out I knew nothing, but with the experience I've gained over the years, this once-shy kid now has the knowledge and ability to write books, anchor corporate events and help people get what it takes to sizzle on stage. I am not bragging when I say this, I just want to reassure you that you are learning from someone who has learned his skill in the trenches. I'm no better than you or anybody else; I am just a little crazier about finding what works and what does not work during a presentation. This knowledge helps me simplify the process so that I can pass it along to you so that you, too, can succeed in public speaking.

This book is a way to simplify things for you to start speaking like a PRO. Let me be clear. This book is for BEGINNERS who want to speak like a PRO. In fact, this book is a very concise version of my book *The Ultimate Public Speaking Survival Guide*, which addresses the 37 biggest public speaking questions of anyone taking a stage. However, do not get carried away by the simplicity or the style of this book. If you implement and take the content seriously, you will be far ahead of many people. In this book, we follow six simple steps to sizzle on stage. First, we will focus on overcoming anxiety, then we'll learn how to prepare, practice and present, finally we'll aim to take it to the next level by understanding strategies for connection and handling glitches.

Let us get started!

Thanks

Rama

1

How to Overcome Public Speaking Anxiety

To be honest, everybody gets anxious when it comes to public speaking. Trust me, even celebrities get nervous. The moment we speak to a group of people, somehow, for some reason we feel the fear. Let us see the root causes of public speaking fear.

ROOT CAUSES OF FEAR OF PUBLIC SPEAKING:

Fundamentally there are two root causes. They are:

Hardwired Fears: The fear of public speaking can be considered a natural response to an overwhelming social situation. The fear of public speaking can be partially hardwired into the human psyche. Considering the conditions of a public speaking event, there is little wonder why the body has such a profound reaction to the situation. One person faces a crowd. The fundamental message for speakers is that there is a danger in the immediate surroundings and they need to protect themselves.

It stands to reason that the body would naturally go into a flight-or-fight response when faced with such a situation. Though you may know that the audience is harmless, you still feel a natural tendency to protect yourself. This makes the fear of public speaking universal to some degree.

Learned Fears: Our early experiences teach us to be afraid of various objects and situations. As a child, you may not be afraid of a flame until you touch one by mistake or just for fun. Or you might have become afraid after seeing someone else get hurt. It is important to remember that the mind is a very powerful force that has a profound effect on our fears. The same applies to public speaking. A negative incident can have lifelong implications. In my short story at the start, I had a bad experience in front of a crowd. The intense fear was felt for just a moment, but the impact lasted pretty long. Hence that intense fear was a learned fear.

Even if the incident is small, you might avoid speaking in public. But if you do, the intensity of the fear will increase and build into a form of glossophobia, which is severe fear of public speaking.

You can really help yourself if you have an answer to the following:

Do you have a phobia?

OR

Do you just have fears?

Fear: Fear is an emotion that is typically hardwired into our beings to ensure our safety. The body has a prominent response to this emotion. This is the reason why we see those physical changes occurring in our bodies when the fear of public speaking starts creeping in. The autonomic nervous system kicks into gear accompanied by the adrenal glands. You know what I am talking about – trembling, repeated gesturing and rapid breathing are common signs. Increased heart rate, sweating and dry mouth can also accompany this emotion.

Overcoming Fear of Public Speaking

I think if you are a regular person with hardwired fears and with a certain extent of learned fears, then your fear of public speaking essentially boils down to fear of uncertainty. By following the steps outlined in this book, you can become certain and confident about your public speaking ability. The more comfortable you get on stage, the sooner you'll overcome your fear.

Phobia: A phobia, such as glossophobia, is a very specific fear that is excessive. Phobias make you seem unreasonable. The mere thought of presentation might get you into a state of intense inaction.

There are fundamental differences between fears and phobias. Our fears are necessary components to self-preservation. They may seem a little unreasonable at times but they do not interfere with our ability to function normally on a day-to-day basis. To put it in simple terms, people may be afraid to deliver an oral presentation. They may perspire, shake and lose their train of thought but definitely will be able to attend the event. They may choose to back out of the speech out of fear but are still quite capable. But if they have a phobia, then the mere thought of giving the presentation will lead to intense physical reactions, anxiety and inaction.

Overcoming Phobia of Public Speaking

If you feel you have a phobia, a viable solution is to take therapy. If you are serious, please follow the following tips while looking for a therapist.

- Look for a therapist who excels in cognitive behavioral therapy and hypnotherapy.
- Check for the success of the therapist. Have they been successful in helping their clients to overcome the phobia?
- When you contact them for your problem, ask them for a sample session. If you are happy with the approach, only then go for the therapy sessions.
- If travel is a problem, check if Skype sessions can be arranged.

Now, let us learn about the Three Pillars of Public Speaking.

2

How to Master the Three Pillars of Public Speaking

Public speaking is nothing but speaking in an amplified manner to more than one person. Some define it as "amplified conversation." Anything or everything that is related to presenting can be traced to one of the following three areas, which are the Three Pillars of Public Speaking:

Your Audience

Your Content

Your Venue

1. YOUR AUDIENCE:

Your presentation is all about what your audience needs. There are usually specific and generic needs of the audience. To find the *specific needs* of your audience, you need to research. The following points can help you with this research. Try to ask potential questions your audience might have regarding your topic and try to answer them as part of your presentation.

Do the audience members belong to a particular age group? Are they college students, corporate employees, younger students, or retired people?

What is the expertise level of your audience in your topic?

What are the shared experiences of your audience?

From my analysis of almost all kinds of presentations, the *generic needs* of any audience can be boiled down to the following items.

- They want to have fun.
- They want to improve their life.
- They want clarity.

2. YOUR CONTENT:

Your content has to be created and then customized. We need to create content based on audience-specific needs and then customize according to audience-generic needs.

Guidelines to *Create the Content*: Have a clear opening, subpoints and supporting points; summarize the points; and have a clear conclusion for your presentation. An illustration would be as shown below.

Opening

Context Setting

Point 1

Supporting point 1

Supporting point 2

Point 2

Supporting point 1

Supporting point 2

....

....

Summarize the points.

Conclusion

If you want to create speeches quickly, download the ready-to-go speech templates from the bonus page for this book. Visit http://publicspeakking.com/essentials.

The following three rules will help you write better.

Use simple words. When we say simple words, it should be words that are used in regular communication and are short syllable words. Anyone hearing the sentence should get the meaning at once.

Use active voice. Active voice is easier to follow and comprehend than passive voice. Our hearing is tuned to listen to active voice.

Use rhetorical devices. These are tools to simplify the meaning. The most common rhetorical devices are:

1. Similes: Comparing a lesser-known concept to a common concept with the use of the word "like." Example: He stood like a rock.

2. Metaphors: A stronger version of simile. Instead of comparing, we refer a concept or a person to another entity. Example: He is a rock.

Steps to *Customize the Content* based on generic needs of the audience.

Generic need 1**:** They want to have fun.

If you want your audience to have fun then, entertain them. You can entertain them by adding humor. Following are some strategies to add humor to your presentation:

Be true and honest: People will have fun if you are true and say things from a unique perspective. For example, I was anchoring an event for my account. Account had funded the event, so my opening statement was: "Ladies and gentlemen, take a break from work and enjoy the evening as much as you can. Why? You never know when such an event would happen again." My audience laughed because it was true that the account had contributed for such an event after a long time and we really did not know when it would sponsor more such events!

Use personal stories: Looking for jokes on the Internet and adding them to your presentation is the last thing you should do. Your audience will love you if you use personal stories which have self-deprecating humor. Self-deprecating humor is making fun of yourself and experiences which you had. For example, once our company executive vice president said during a talk, "I said to my wife, 'I am going to lead the new business unit in the company.' She said, 'Okay.' I said, 'Aren't you happy?'

She asked, 'Okay tell me, will you get more money or not?'" It might or might not sound funny but during the event he sounded hilarious because he was the unit head and he was very open about the experience.

Use your physicality: If you are tall or short, dark or fair, find ways to relate it somewhere in your presentation. It will work like magic. Trust me, it is an easy way to create humor.

If you are serious about learning more about creating humor, you can refer to my book *Connect Using Humor and Story*, where I detail how I got 18 laughs and 3 rounds of applause in a 7-minute persuasive speech.

Generic need 2: They want to improve their life.

The very reason you are giving a presentation is because your audience is willing to listen. The only way we can honor them is by presenting content that will help them. One of the strategies to achieve the same is to structure your presentation in E-P-A (experience, point, application).

Experience: It could be transmitted using various mediums. The most common tool is use of story. Two other tools are adding statistics and adding relevant citations from leaders or experts in the area of your topic.

Point: What is the lesson from the story? How did it make a difference?

Application: How can the lesson be applied in the life of your audience?

The above structure not only works for speaking in the community world but also in the corporate world – whether it is a sales presentation, technical presentation, or a speech to boost team performance.

If you need some suggestions for how to come up with stories or ideas to inspire the audience, please check out the blog http://PublicSpeakKing.com/inspirational-speech or refer to *Public Speaking Topic Secrets.*

Generic need 3**:** They want CLARITY.

By far I think the most important part in your content preparation is the CLARITY of your presentation.

Answer the following questions:

What is the single message that my audience will take back home?

Are the transitions clear for me to go from one point to another?

Are my stories, data and statistics in tune with my core message?

There is a simple tool to check if your content is CLEAR. This is something that I learned from Lance Miller, 2005 World Champion of Public Speaking. I am sure it applies to every presentation. For a presentation, we use either verbal (words) or non-verbal (body language, visual aids) communication.

The problem?

We might start rambling too much information. To create a clear presentation that will be memorable for our audience, we need to understand the "Painting the Picture" technique. The technique is to paint the audience's mind with the same picture that you are seeing in your mind. As communicators, our aim is to transfer the picture we have in our mind to our audience's mind. One way to create clear content is to look at each verbal and non-verbal aspect of our presentation and ask, "If I am in the audience, will this sentence or action paint the exact picture?"

If the answer is yes, we will keep the action or sentence. If not, we need to chuck it out. Why? If you are not clear, how can you expect someone else to be clear?

This tool will help you to find the right words or actions (whether to use movement or specific gestures, use PowerPoint or flipcharts, etc.). This will lead you to choose the best elements for an effective communication process.

3. YOUR VENUE:

The setting for your presentation is the third pillar of a presentation. It is your responsibility to get the venue in tune for maximum effectiveness. Venue plays an important role in the success of your presentation. If you have direct access to it, work with the presentation planner well ahead of your actual presentation day on the following points.

Six Factors at Venue That Can Affect Your Performance:

1. Venue Type: Is your setting going to be boardroom style where the audience will number somewhere from 10 to 40? Is the setting going to be classroom style where the approximate audience size will be somewhere from 40 to 100? Is the setting going to be auditorium style, which is ideal for a large audience, greater than 100? *Knowing this will help you visualize the venue while you are practicing.*

2. Time Limit: Do you have a time limit? Are you going to be timed by someone in the audience or will you manage it by yourself? These questions will help you prepare your presentation from a time limit perspective. You can cut down the number of words depending on time limit. For example, if you have been given 10 minutes, then you can plan to have 1200 to 1400 words based on the rate of your speech. You can also be prepared for an emergency ending, just in case you are asked to speak for less time.

3. Projector: If you are using Microsoft PowerPoint or Apple Keynote, or any DIGITAL VISUAL AID, check if the venue has a projector. If not, make sure you have alternatives such as chart boards. You can also buy a pocket projector if that'll help you. PK301 PICO projector is a good option.

4. Audience Seating Position: They can be in boardroom, conference room or dinner table style. Boardroom is where there is a big table and the audience members are sitting around the circumference of the table. Conference type is where seats are arranged in rows and columns. Dinner style is where the audience is around circular dining tables. From personal experience, dinner style is not a good setup from the speaker's point of view. The reasons are:

- The audience is not seated in a pattern for making connection through eye contact.
- The audience seems scattered and the energy is unevenly spread across the venue.

How can you make audience seating work to your advantage? Ask the meeting planner to put out only as many chairs as per the confirmed participation. The remaining chairs can be in a stacked position and can be added if more people turn out. The rule of thumb is: *Never leave empty chairs for a presentation.* Energy dissipates in emptiness. On the other hand, if the chairs/ tables are close, then there is a sense of connection and energy in the room, which will boost the overall atmosphere of the venue.

5. Acoustics: Acoustics of the venue matters. A venue with good acoustics will transmit sound clearly so that it is easy for the listener. If you have a chance, check the acoustics of the venue beforehand. If you are not happy with the acoustics and you have a choice, you can check with the presentation planner for a work-around.

6. Audibility: As your audience size increases, you need to take care of another critical factor, which is your AUDIBILITY. Don't worry if you do not have a low, deep and resonant voice. We have tools such as a MICROPHONE to solve this issue. With a mid-size audience setting, use of a microphone is optional. To determine if a microphone is necessary, run a simple test. Go to the venue before the presentation date. Ask your friend or colleague to sit in the corners of the venue. Speak in your normal voice. If the room acoustics are good, you will be audible to your friend. If not, you need to use a microphone.

Check if you have a microphone available at the venue. Learn which microphone is suitable for you. Is it a clip-on microphone or a handheld mike? If you are not comfortable with a handheld mike, then ask the planner to arrange a clip-on microphone. If you are using a clip-on microphone, you might clip it on your suit collar. I would not recommend it because your voice might get distorted if you use amplified gestures. For men, clipping the microphone on your tie would be a neat idea. For both men and women, clipping the microphone between the first and second button of your shirt would be ideal.

3

How to Practice For the Presentation Day

You know, at a high level, public speaking seems to be a simple process. You speak and your audience listens – that's it? Maybe it is not that simple. That's the reason I have created a simple step-by-step process to act as a one-stop reference for your practice. Note: As you progress down the steps, do not forget to incorporate the lessons of the earlier steps.

20 Steps for an Effective Practice Session:

1. Stand straight with firm footing. Keep your spine and head straight.
2. Keep your hands at your sides with your fingers slightly curled.
3. Keep your feet 8 to 12 inches apart from each other.
4. At this point, you need not worry about eye contact, gesturing, movement, facial expressions or voice modulation.

5. Practice your speech content till it smoothly rolls off your tongue. Certain sentences or words might not be rolling off smoothly. Go back to your content and change the words or sentences that are not rolling off smoothly. You can keep doing this activity throughout your preparation phase.

6. Check for any distracting mechanisms in your current speech. If you find any, work on removing them by practicing for specific non-verbal or verbal behavior.

7. Practice by speaking your content in loud, soft, slow and last of all fast tones. While doing so, take care that you also enunciate (make sure you end the words properly, saying each syllable of every word) the words clearly. By doing this step, you will clear vocal blocks, sound clear and use optimum tone.

8. Complete every word before you go to the next word.

9. Check if you are not starting the sentences in high energy and ending in low energy. If the content demands it, it's okay. However, if it is a regular pattern, practice to break that pattern.

10. Now start focusing on internalizing your speech. You should be able to tell the content even if someone wakes you up in the middle of the night. This is the concept of muscle memory.

11. If you are planning to pause at certain places in your talk, then practice those pauses deliberately.

12. Feel the emotion in your heart and practice. If your content should make your audience feel happy, you should also feel the happiness. If your content should get your audience excited, you should also be excited.

13. Ask your friend to give feedback on relevance of your facial expressions to the intent of your speech.

14. Work on your eye contact by visualizing strategy. Imagine the audience spread across different quadrants. Say you divide the audience into four different quadrants. Talk to one person in quadrant one and complete your idea or sentence. Then, move to a different quadrant. Now, talk to that person and complete your idea or sentence. Similarly do this for all quadrants. You can repeat this cycle – however, make sure you see a different person in each quadrant.

15. Let your hand gestures flow naturally. Practice the following rules of thumb:

    a. Use open palms.

    b. Do not point at the audience.

    c. Move hands from shoulder level.

    d. Stroke at the right word.

16. Work on your movements. Check your footwork; determine at what point of the stage you would be at different parts of your presentation.
17. If you are using PowerPoint, practice by sequencing the slides. You can practice by asking your friend to navigate the slides for you. Alternatively, you can use a remote control for the same.
18. Now, rehearse by incorporating all the steps. This is the fun part. It might be boring at times. At one point, you will feel powerful and excited. This is when you know you are evolving as a successful speaker.
19. Give a complete rehearsal to your close friends, family or anyone who would listen to your presentation.
20. Keep repeating the steps and fine-tune your presentation.

The above strategy is not something specific to a newcomer. It will work and help you even if you are a fairly seasoned speaker. I have learned that the above steps are kind of THE work you need to do if you really want to speak like a PROFESSIONAL.

A strategy for not going blank on stage:

Going blank on the stage is one of the main fears of public speaking. Let's talk about it. There is general advice such as "You should not over prepare your presentation." Well, the reason for this advice is that you might look scripted or artificial. Moreover, you can easily go blank if you do not recall the script word by word. But that is generic advice. We are talking about specificity. I think you should over prepare your presentation. When I say over prepare, I mean drill (or internalize) the speech till the content becomes part of you. If I wake you up in the middle of your sleep and ask you to talk about your presentation, you should talk. We are not talking about storing it in memory. We are talking about storing it in your muscles. *Your aim is to take your speech to* MUSCLE MEMORY. When you do this, there is genuine excitement. When you are at that state, there is no question of going blank. You will be telling yourself – "I can't wait to give my presentation." This is one of the simplest ways to get over your anxiety and sizzle on stage. You do this – and I bet you will be excited to go on stage.

4

How to Handle the Presentation Day

Presentation day is the D-Day. First of all, you need energy to show energy in your presentation! Eat light food. Breads and salads will work fine. The second thing: If you are going to use a laptop, make sure it is fully charged but still take your charger. If you have a PowerPoint presentation or videos to present, have a backup in a pen drive and in a DVD. Third thing: Dress sharp: If you are not sure what to wear, follow this rule of thumb. Dress up one step further than the best-dressed person in your audience. Finally, hang around with a supportive friend. You need someone to bounce your content onto. You will feel less stressed if there is a dependable person with you.

I have collated a list of simple additional things that will help you to give a splendid presentation.

1. Reach the venue as early as possible and meet the presentation planner. He or she should help you with the setting. If there is no planner as such, you need to take charge and check on the following points:

a. Is the projector working? If you have a PowerPoint presentation, is it getting displayed through the projector?

b. If a white board is needed, check for its condition and a working marker.

c. Are the chairs arranged properly? Is the number of chairs in accordance with the number of people who have confirmed their attendance?

d. Do you have the right temperature set up for air-conditioning?

2. If you are going to use a microphone, test for the optimum sound. You can ask your friend or colleague to sit in different corners of the room and give feedback about your voice clarity. Do this activity by placing the microphone at varying distances from your mouth.

3. Is there any light that is focused on the speaker? Do you want it on or off?

4. Are the lights working in the room? Do you want the lights to be on or off?

5. Remind the presentation planner or the anchor to ask the audience members to keep their cell phones on silent.

6. If you have an introduction, hand over a copy to the planner or anchor.

7. By the time you are done with the setting, your audience might start walking into the venue. You can connect with your audience even before you start speaking by:

    a. Reaching out to members and greeting them, while having a genuine smile.

    b. Complimenting them. It could be as simple as "Nice shirt," "Nice tie," "Love your smile," etc.

    c. Genuinely conversing with them. Ask what brings them there or what they are expecting. Keep it quick and move on. It should not appear that you are trying this deliberately. It has to be natural.

8. Suppose 10 minutes before your presentation, you are feeling nervous. You can use the following technique to overcome the nervousness. Rub your right palm with your left hand and vice versa for 10 to 15 seconds. Then do slow breathe-in and breathe-out till your heart rate is normal. Have a mindset of fun and excitement. Think about your intent of the presentation and the very reason you are going on the stage.

9. When you are called upon, go to the stage with enthusiasm. Smile and pause for a few seconds before you start. Your pause will do two things. First, the audience will start focusing on you. Second, the audience will develop a connection with you. Go ahead and enjoy your presentation!

10. During the presentation, be present, be passionate and exhibit energy.
11. After the presentation, take feedback from the audience.

Now, let us see some simple yet effective ways to connect with our audience.

5

How to Create a Connection With the Audience

I am sure you have heard or used the term "connection." For example, "I felt a connection with him" or ''I did not connect with him," etc. I have realized that the sooner the audience members feel your CREDIBILITY, the faster your connection will be. The following will help you create a connection with your audience.

Six Practical Tools for Creating a Connection:

1. Your Introduction: In most instances, you will be invited to present on stage by an anchor or a master of ceremonies. If you are talking to a new audience, then your introduction plays a crucial role in building likeability and trust. It is your responsibility to share your introduction in a way that covers the following points:

What expertise do you bring to the table or in other words, why you are qualified to speak?

Care should be taken that the introduction does not involve ego boosting such as speaker "climbed Mt. Everest in one hour," speaker "has a triple Ph.D.," speaker "ran a 10-mile marathon in 2 minutes" etc. The examples are extreme forms but I hope you get the idea.

The introduction should address how you are going to help the audience. It's also good to include something about you that is not related to your topic.

Take the following introduction as an example: "There is a concept and method by which you can create a joke. Once you know this, you can bring life into your presentations. This concept and method helped our speaker to be among the top entertaining speakers at the national level. And today he is going to teach us 'How to Create Humor.' He likes jaywalking in Times Square and eats cupcakes when he gets stressed. Are you ready to listen? Please join me in welcoming Mr.............."

2. Use the Pronouns You/We: I learned this tool from 1999 World Champion of Public Speaking Craig Valentine. The idea is to have as many "you" focused sentences as possible. Let me explain. When we speak, we bring our own experiences and achievements to the table and there is a tendency to use "I." While creating content, you need to frame it in such a way that you transition and involve the audience using "you" or "we" focused sentences so they understand that you care about them. In fact, if you have noticed, I tend to use more "you" or "we" even in this book.

3. Speak in the Third Person: Whenever you use "I," think twice. Unless it is your own original thought, realization, finding, experience or learning, do not use "I." If the idea or teaching is someone else's, use that person in the reference. For example, when talking about ethos, logos and pathos, I clearly mentioned that it was a concept coined by Aristotle. The speaker's job is only to simplify and spread the information. This helps in establishing your credibility.

4. Be Sincere: Sincerely add value to your audience's life experience. Adding value could vary based on the purpose of your speech. If you are there to entertain them, give your 100% in entertaining them. If you are there to train them for project management skills, empower them to become the best project managers. If you are there to inspire them, genuinely help them to achieve greater things in life.

5. Maintain Genuine Eye Contact: Eyes are doorways to form a connection. Not just in public speaking but even in one-on-one communications, we form connections through our eyes. While presenting, there is a tendency to glaze over them, but the moment you talk *with* an audience, you develop a deeper bonding. The mechanics is explained in point 14 of "20 Steps for An Effective Practice Session."

6. Engage Your Audience: If your presentation has scope, you can use audience engagement to keep your audience interested throughout your presentation. When you involve someone, they will listen to you all day long. Engage your audience with the following ideas.

Ask interactive questions: By asking interactive questions, you get immediate feedback on your audience's understanding of your subject. You can create a pop quiz, ask questions about them or ask questions about what you just explained.

Invite a few of them to the stage: This is a great technique if you are conducting workshops or training sessions. This way you have caught the attention of all the members because one of them is hanging out with you in the spotlight (so to speak).

Create a group activity: By doing this, the audience members interact with each other and work as a team. This works great for workshops or training sessions.

6

How to Handle Glitches During the Presentation

During a live speech, situations could arise which were not planned. They can either fluster you or you can use them to your advantage.

The best possible way to handle problems is to be aware of the current situation. The #1 rule is *not to get flustered.* Know that your audience will empathize if there is a problem and always want you to do well. So, respect that and continue with your presentation.

Let us see the possible problems that you might face during your presentation.

Losing Train of Thought: While giving your presentation, you might lose your train of thought. It could happen because you saw someone and got distracted, or you were unsettled, or you were just anxious. If this happens, please do not kick yourself. Let me give an example. I was supposed to speak at 5:45 p.m. Saturday. The meeting started at 5 p.m. I started from my home, picked up a few friends and hit the road to the venue. However, I reached the venue parking at 5:42 p.m. (thanks to the insane amount of traffic!). I reached the meeting hall at 5:45 p.m. exactly. Before I could even adjust to the new climate, I started with my opening. "I know Jim since 2009. At that time, he was a big man. Even now he is a big man, physically. To describe Jim in one line – Jim is like a 120-liter Coca-Cola bottle opening happiness wherever he goes." After that, I was supposed to say, *"Jim did not pay me to say this. He is a great trainer and an awesome coach. You can contact him if you want coaching for prepared speeches, impromptu speeches or finding a girlfriend."* But because of the hustle and bustle, I lost my train of thought and missed it. However, I had a stock line to use. I said, "That's it. I am done." People laughed. It gave me time to get back on track.

Strategies for bouncing back:

Have some stock lines that can be used in case you lose your train of thought.

Even if you forget, do not try to go back and share the missed portion. The joke I missed was a great one. However, I did not go back or try to force it into the later part of the talk.

Remember the structure, instead of words. If you do so, you'll know at which point of the presentation you were. Hence, you'll move on with your presentation.

Power Shuts Down: If power shuts down or PowerPoint does not work, just be cool. When this happens, your microphone might turn off and/or your PowerPoint might stop. You can use this opportunity to say something light such as "So I will always be in the limelight" or "Was this is a plan to test my presentation skills?"

This once happened in our corporate town hall. The entire power supply went off except for the microphone. The speaker said, "The microphone works. So, I will continue. My forehead can probably reflect the light you need." He was bald. The entire house erupted with laughter.

If you are halfway through the presentation and power shuts down, you can say, "I think we need a break."

Cell Phone Ringing: This is a very common scenario. You can be prepared with an answer or two. If you feel it did not disturb the flow of your presentation, you can ignore it. If you feel it did, you can keep few lines ready to create humor. For instance, Craig Valentine in one of his audio programs used the following stock line: "Please tell your friend that I will call him later."

Latecomer to Your Presentation: Someone walking in late to your presentation is a common scenario. In that case, you can choose to ignore it and act as if nothing happened. This is a good idea if the person sneaked in without disturbing the flow of your presentation. In some cases, the person might hamper the flow of your presentation. In such cases, you can tease around the person and create humor. Stand-up comedians use the following lines in such situations: "Welcome, we were just waiting for you" or "Do you need something… like a watch?"

Conclusion

I know you could have picked from dozens of books on public speaking but you took a chance on mine. Thank you for reading and completing this book.

Please do not underestimate the information given in this book. It is distilled enough to give you on-point information on how to overcome your anxiety and speak with confidence onstage.

Public speaking doesn't need to be hard. Really, it's simple if you follow the steps I just detailed. The whole process can be simplified into six steps.

1. Accept that fear of public speaking is okay. It is natural.
2. Know your audience, your content and your venue.
3. Prepare for your presentation – practice, practice, and practice.
4. Present with excitement and energy.
5. Strive to connect with your audience.
6. Be prepared to handle glitches.

Imagine you presenting in style at your job, or in your community or classroom. People will start respecting you and you'll be seen as an authority in your designated area.

However, becoming good at public speaking requires work. I hope you understand that nothing worthwhile comes easy. Follow each of these action items and start speaking like a PRO.

If you have feedback or want to share your thoughts, please reach out to me at Rama@PublicSpeakking.com. I'll do my best to respond.

Keep Smiling, Keep Rocking and Happy Public Speaking

Wish You Success,
Ramakrishna Reddy

Made in the USA
Monee, IL
02 July 2020